Dear American Girl,

Ever since I was a girl, I've lo_____iffy P's,
elegant *Y*'s and *G*'s, an_____ed
sending silly notes, special po_____. So
writing this book was especia_____t
reading it will be just as much fun for you.

I've included lots of great ways to play with paper and pencil—
and markers, and scissors, and glue, and old maps, and
bananas, and, well, just about anything. You can use these
ideas whether you're leaving a note on the fridge, writing a long
letter to a faraway friend, decorating a book report cover, or
just getting crafty on a rainy afternoon!

I hope you'll have fun experimenting with all these ways to
doodle, write, and create special deliveries. But most of all, I
hope my ideas will inspire you to discover even more ways of
putting your unique stamp on everything you write.

Your pen pal,

Laura Allen

Table of Contents

Clever Lettering

Play with the way you put words on a page—or a report cover, a poster, a card, even a graham cracker! Or just have some fun doodling in your notebook. 6

TOP SECRET

Psssst! Peek inside this secret section to find crafty codes, invisible inks, and other sneaky ways to keep your special messages PRIVATE! 24

Paper Capers

Surprise your friends with these paper pranks—everything from Post-it® patchworks to fabulous "fan" mail. 40

IT'S TIME TO TAKE
THE I-DOT CHALLENGE!
Before you read any further,
get out a piece of scrap paper
and see how many different
ways you can dot an **i**.
Then turn the page...

This is a real **I**-opener, isn't it?
Did you draw any of the same i-dots that I did?

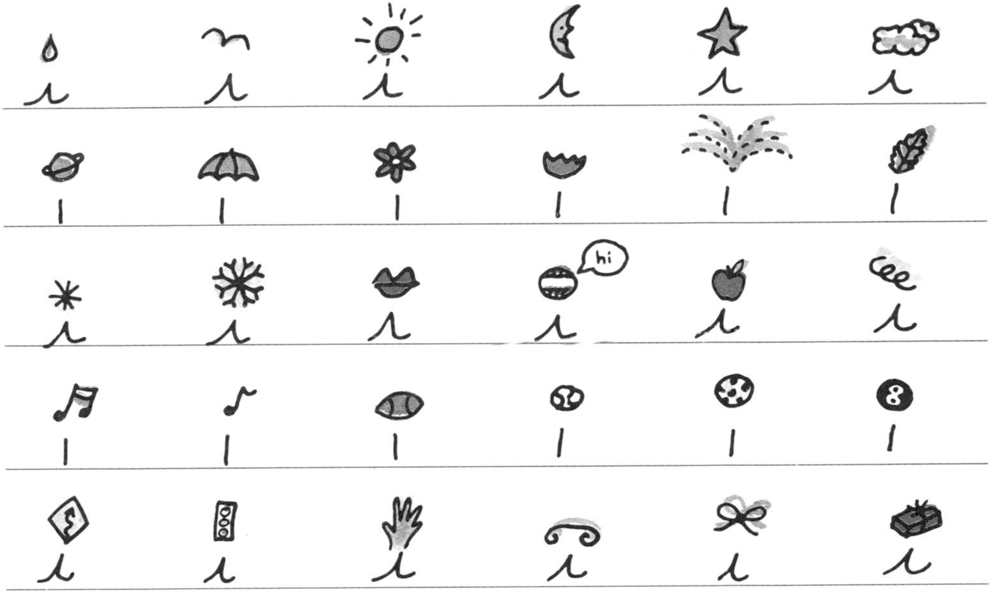

Now, don't forget to cross your

and fill in your  . Do you know why the final e is silent? Because it's "sleep-e"!

And while you're at it,

you might want to make a curly-  too!

nine

Get really stylish with . . .

dotting!

You can put dots at the beginnings and ends of the lines, like

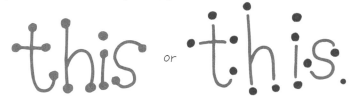

this or ·t·h·i·s·

Other shapes are also fun to play with. See?

TRIANGLES
SQUARES

You can also dot all the way around each letter, but that takes much more

time.

8

Doubling

is something you can do anytime. You just need two different-colored pens, markers, or pencils, and a little concentration. Write what you want to double. Then, using another color, retrace your original strokes.

Twins or Twiims

Stay right next to the lines.

Leave a gap between them.

What do you think?
Are you ready to try Triiplliing?

How about doubled scriiptt?

For a fun giggle, make your words

wiggle!

Make hot words red. Make cold words blue.

Let wet words splash or drip onto

you

Put  **6ubbles** in your **6ath** and

 **music** in your notes.

TIP: Having bubble trouble? Draw a tiny tic-tac-toe board with curved lines.

Add  **sparkle** to

stars and **snowflakes.**

A plus sign (+) with an X through it makes a twinkle. Add short lines for rays of light.

You can turn twinkles into snowflakes by adding V's to their ends.

Just  **picture** what you wrote!

Friday
13

Create an
Alphabet
Art Gallery.

Just draw each letter of the alphabet in the shape of something that begins with that letter. Use a dictionary if you need ideas.

Try out your ideas on scrap paper.

B is for Blue.

Nope—
too boring!

B is for Bluebird.

That's better.

REMEMBER:
Every idea is worth trying.
After all, there's no telling where it might lead.

15

You can **Pretty** up your printing just by putting **Patterns** in it!

Special letters are great for:
-  your initials or your name,
- fancy titles on school report covers,
- the first letter of a new sentence or paragraph.

16

Collectible Letters

There are lots of cool characters out there, so why not clip them out and use them to dress up reports, posters, and cards?

TIP: A good way to store your collection is in a photo album with peel-back pages. Then you can pull the letters out and place them, copy them, or trace them.

17

To make your printing pop out, try
SHADOWING IT!

Step 1 Use pencil to draw a letter in outline form.

Step 2 Draw the same letter again, overlapping your first. Be sure to match all the lines and curves exactly.

Step 3 Erase any lines that cross through the second letter you drew. This makes one letter look like it's behind the other.

Step 4 Use black to fill in the part of the letter in back that still shows. Fill in the front with a different color.

Imagine your letters are cardboard cutouts with a light shining on them. Picture where the shadows would fall and what they'd look like.

If you can't picture this, why not try it with a real flashlight and a cutout letter?

BIG IMPORTANT TIP:
Your shadows will look more realistic if they all go in the **same** direction instead of **different** ones.

Once you've mastered shadowing, try

Building Blocks.

TIP: For practice, use tracing paper to trace these block letters.

Step 1

Draw the letters of your word in outline form.

Step 2

Draw the same letters again, overlapping the first ones. Make sure you match all lines and curves.

Step 3

Connect the edges of your front and back letters.

Step 4

Erase the lines you wouldn't see if each letter were a solid block of wood.

Step 5

Add shading. Fill in lighter colors first so you don't wind up with streaks where you've touched darker lines.

That's Funny!

TIP: Block letters are big, so plan ahead! Lightly sketch evenly spaced dashes for your letters to sit on.

21

How would you like to EAT your things?

Colored icing that comes in tubes at the grocery store is great for writing.

For a sweet telegram, why not "tell-a-graham?" All you need is sugar glue and some decorative toppings.

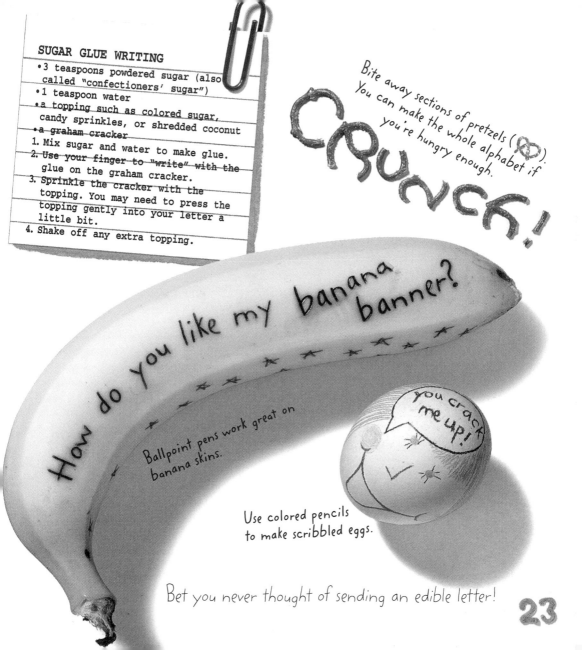

SUGAR GLUE WRITING

- 3 teaspoons powdered sugar (also called "confectioners' sugar")
- 1 teaspoon water
- a topping such as colored sugar, candy sprinkles, or shredded coconut
- a graham cracker

1. Mix sugar and water to make glue.
2. Use your finger to "write" with the glue on the graham cracker.
3. Sprinkle the cracker with the topping. You may need to press the topping gently into your letter a little bit.
4. Shake off any extra topping.

Bite away sections of pretzels (🥨). You can make the whole alphabet if you're hungry enough.

CRUNCH!

How do you like my banana banner?

Ballpoint pens work great on banana skins.

you crack me up!

Use colored pencils to make scribbled eggs.

Bet you never thought of sending an edible letter!

23

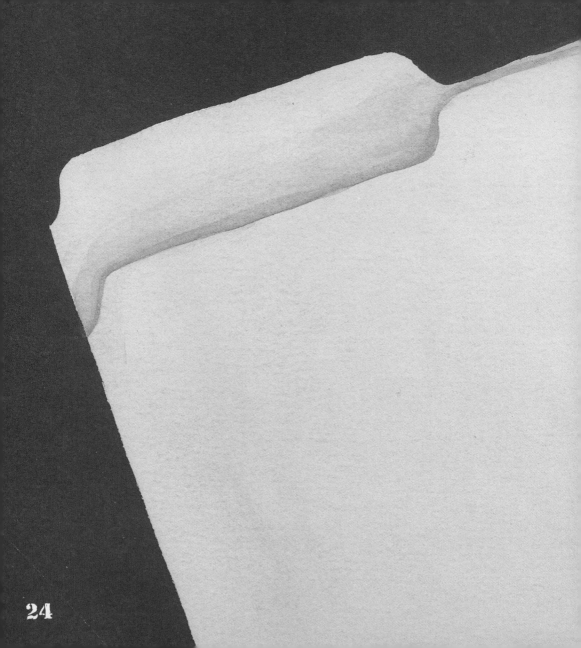

25

Write with white.

A white crayon or candle can be a crafty tool for writing secret notes. You can't see the message until you paint over it with watercolors or color over it with a highlighter.

White Crayon

Here's another *juicy* secret.

You can write with fresh or bottled lemon juice. It's nearly *invisible* until you heat it.

To write a lemon letter . . .

all you need are lemon juice, a small paintbrush, and white paper. Dip the brush in the juice, paint your message, and let it dry before you send it.

On the envelope leave a clue, so your friend knows what to do.

To read a lemon letter . . .

all you need is a lightbulb that's turned on. Hold the paper next to the bulb until letters appear. Slowly, move the paper until you are able to see the whole message.

Make a great impression.

This kind of writing is invisible until you rub it with pencil.

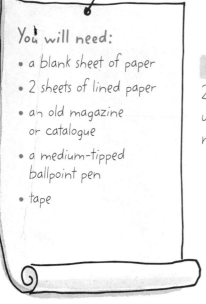

You will need:

- a blank sheet of paper
- 2 sheets of lined paper
- an old magazine or catalogue
- a medium-tipped ballpoint pen
- tape

Step 1 Place your blank paper between the 2 sheets of lined paper with all the edges lined up. Then lay the papers on the catalogue or magazine and tape them down.

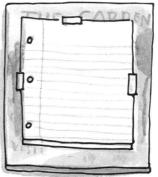

A magazine will keep you from carving your message into your desk. The bottom piece of lined paper will keep the magazine ink from transferring onto the back of your message.

Step 2 Use the ballpoint pen to write your message on the lined paper, pressing as hard as you can.

Step 3 Carefully peel the lined paper off the top. Give the "blank" sheet to a friend who knows to rub over it lightly with the side of a pencil.

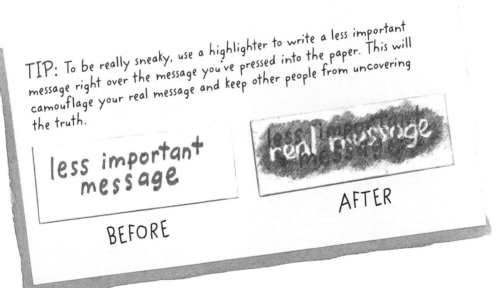

TIP: To be really sneaky, use a highlighter to write a less important message right over the message you've pressed into the paper. This will camouflage your real message and keep other people from uncovering the truth.

less important message

BEFORE

real message

AFTER

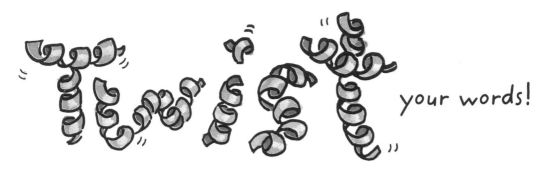
Twist your words!

You will need:

- a sheet of paper
- scissors
- a pencil to wrap
- a pencil for writing
- 2 small rubber bands

Step 1 Cut a long, thin strip of paper ¼ inch wide (about as wide as a pencil).

Step 2 Attach one end of your strip to the end of one pencil by wrapping a rubber band around it. Spiral the paper around the pencil so that the paper's edges touch without overlapping. (You might have to crinkle the paper at the beginning.)

Step 3 When you get to the end of the paper, rubber-band it down.

Step 4 Write a short message across the pencil. Make sure you line up the letters evenly as you go across, and leave a blank space between words. When you get to the end, even if you're in the middle of a word, turn the pencil a little bit and continue writing underneath the letters you just wrote.

Circle the first letter of your message.

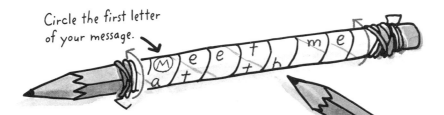

Step 5 When you've finished, remove the rubber bands and straighten out the strip. Don't worry if the letters look jumbled. They should be!

All your friend needs to decode your message is a pencil the same size as yours to wrap the strip around. Make sure she knows to start wrapping at the circled letter, which is the beginning of your message.

e
u

m
e
o

h
h
t

t
t
e
a

e
e
x.
e
t
r
e
i
Ⓜ
a
t
s
s

Message: Meet me at the treehouse at six.

Try simple substituting.

Use numbers instead of letters. It's as easy as 1-2-3!

Step 1 Write the alphabet in one long row across your paper.

Step 2 Underneath, write the numbers 1—26 in any order.

A	B	C	D	E	F	G	H	I	J	K	L	M	N	O	P	Q	R	S	T	U	V	W	X	Y	Z
5	11	3	4	26	18	6	13	7	2	12	9	15	19	17	23	10	8	25	20	21	16	22	1	14	24

← Draw lines to help you line up the numbers and letters.

Step 3 Use the numbers below each letter to "spell" messages. (Be sure to leave plenty of space around two-digit numbers.)

Can you figure out this message using the numbered alphabet above?

13 5 23 23 14
3 17 4 7 19 6!

Answer: Happy coding!

Change one letter to another. It's as easy as ABC! Or BCD, or CDE, . . .

Step 1 Write the alphabet in small (lowercase) letters in one long row across your paper.

Step 2 Directly below it, write the alphabet again in capital letters, starting with a different letter. For instance:

a	b	c	d	e	f	g	h	i	j	k	l	m	n	o	p	q	r	s	t	u	v	w	x	y	z
H	I	J	K	L	M	N	O	P	Q	R	S	T	U	V	W	X	Y	Z	A	B	C	D	E	F	G

After Z start over with A.

Step 3 To write in your new code, replace each top letter with the one below it. Only people who know the letter you used to start your secret alphabet will be able to decode your messages.

Pssst . . . Why did the spy go out in the rain?

ANSWER:

ZOL DHUALK AV
JHAJO H JVKL!
(OLL OLL)

(Hint: Use the H-code shown in Step 2)

Answer: She wanted to catch a code! (hee hee)

33

Dot marks the spot.

No one will spot your secret message if you leave the letters off the page. Here's how!

Step 1 Write the alphabet in scrambled order across the first line of a sheet of notebook paper. Try to space the letters out evenly.

Step 2 Cut across the paper just below the letters.

I X J C D A G R L Q B K H Y M V O F N T U W P Z S E

Step 3 Place your alphabet strip at the top of another sheet of notebook paper, lining up the top left and right edges exactly.

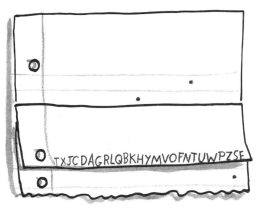

Step 4 Think of a short message to write. Find the first letter of it on the alphabet strip and put a dot under it. Move the strip down one line, find the next letter, and put a dot under it. Keep going, line by line, to finish the message.

Now make your friend an alphabet strip exactly like yours so she can read all your messages.

Step 1 Place your alphabet strip at the top of a new sheet of notebook paper with the left, right, and top edges lined up.

Step 2 Copy your alphabet directly below the strip, matching both the letters and the spacing between them.

Step 3 Cut this new alphabet off the page in one long strip.

more

To read a message, all your friend has to do is slide her alphabet strip down the page one line at a time, writing down the letter that appears above each dot.

Can you figure out what this says?

TIP: You don't have to use dots. Any little doodle will do!

Answer: This is so cool

Partners in Crime

Can you find the hidden message lurking in these letters?

TH EB UD DY SY ST EM IS NO TJ US TF OR
FI EL DT RI PS AN YM OR E!

It's easy to disguise words just by breaking them into pairs of letters.
To decode this kind of message, put the buddies back in single file without any space between them, like this:

THEBUDDYSYSTEMISNOTJUSTFORFIELDTRIPSANYMORE!

KIS (keep it short).

Computer users communicate quickly with these clever abbreviations.
You can use them whether you're writing on-line or on lined paper.

G = grin

BG = big grin

VBG = very big grin

GMTA =
great minds think alike

IC = I see

IMO =
in my opinion

J/K = just
kidding

LOL = laughing out loud

ROFL = rolling on floor laughing

ROFLWTIME =
rolling on floor laughing with tears
in my eyes

F2F = face to face

PU = that stinks

Tx = thanks

MAKE UP
YOUR OWN
ABBREVIATIONS!

Say it with a smiley.

Make silly sideways faces using these symbols on your keyboard.

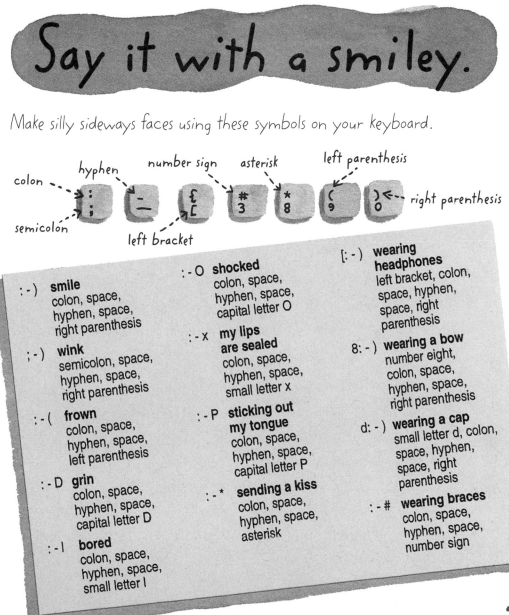

colon

hyphen

number sign

asterisk

left parenthesis

semicolon

left bracket

right parenthesis

: -) smile
colon, space, hyphen, space, right parenthesis

; -) wink
semicolon, space, hyphen, space, right parenthesis

: - (frown
colon, space, hyphen, space, left parenthesis

: - D grin
colon, space, hyphen, space, capital letter D

: - | bored
colon, space, hyphen, space, small letter I

: - O shocked
colon, space, hyphen, space, capital letter O

**: - x my lips
are sealed**
colon, space, hyphen, space, small letter x

**: - P sticking out
my tongue**
colon, space, hyphen, space, capital letter P

: - * sending a kiss
colon, space, hyphen, space, asterisk

**[: -) wearing
headphones**
left bracket, colon, space, hyphen, space, right parenthesis

8: -) wearing a bow
number eight, colon, space, hyphen, space, right parenthesis

d: -) wearing a cap
small letter d, colon, space, hyphen, space, right parenthesis

: - # wearing braces
colon, space, hyphen, space, number sign

the longest letter ever.

Just start your letter at the beginning of the roll and keep writing in one long line until you've run out of paper—or things to say. If you finish your letter before you finish the roll, just cut off the extra paper. Then rewind your letter and secure it with a rubber band.

Be a cut-up!

If you're looking for a humorous way
to ask for something without delay,
try ransom-note writing without the crime.
It's sure to work almost every time.

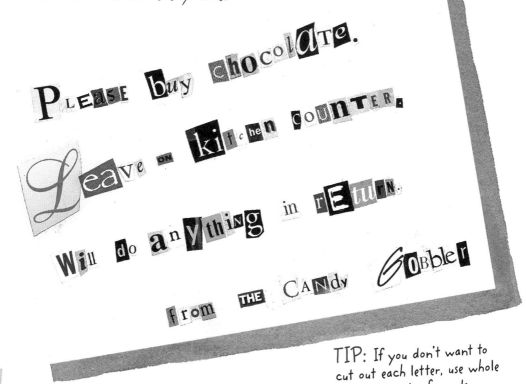

PLEASE buy chocolATe.

Leave on kitchen COUNTER.

Will do anything in rEturn.

from THE CANdy Gobbler

TIP: If you don't want to cut out each letter, use whole words or parts of words.

TIP: To give your note a border like this one, cut it out with pinking shears.

Send a mixed message.

You will need:
- paper
- a pen or pencil
- scissors
- an envelope

Step 1 Write your letter, starting each sentence on a new line. Don't write on the back of the paper.

> Dear Makiko,
> We picked up the new puppy today.
> You'll have to come play with it soon.
> We went out for ice cream afterwards.
> It was delicious.
> How was your cousin's birthday party?
> I can't wait to hear about it.
> Write me soon, OK?
>   Love,
>   Laura

Step 2 Cut the sentences apart. When you're finished, you'll have a pile of strips.

46

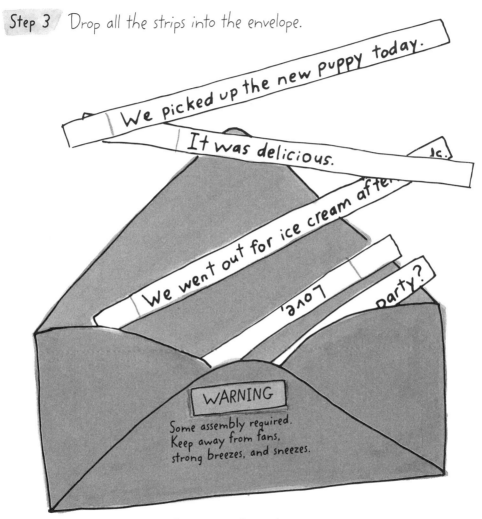

We picked up the new puppy today.

It was delicious.

Jc.

We went out for ice cream after

Love,

party?

WARNING

Some assembly required.
Keep away from fans,
strong breezes, and sneezes.

Write a hint on the outside about the
puzzling pieces inside.

With enough Post-it® Notes, pens, and pals to pitch in, you can perk up a piece of posterboard or newsprint in no time.

Make triangles by cutting square Post-its in half diagonally.

Combine different-shaped Post-its to create fun patterns . . .

or draw your own patterns on the Post-its.

Play Post-it Peekaboo! Write a riddle on top and the answer underneath.

What do you call a puppy with a fever?

a hot dog!

49

Write on the edge.

The edges of your notepads are great places to write special messages to yourself.

Step 1 Bend the pad toward you and write on the fanned-out part.

Step 2 Bend the pad away from you and write on the fanned-out part.

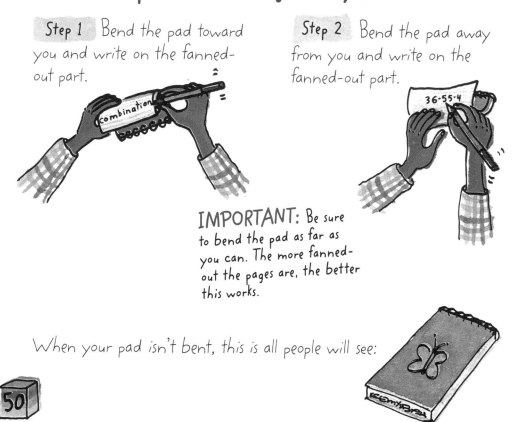

IMPORTANT: Be sure to bend the pad as far as you can. The more fanned-out the pages are, the better this works.

When your pad isn't bent, this is all people will see:

You can hide notes to yourself on the edge of a single sheet of paper, too.

Fold the paper like this. . .

☐ Call Grandpa Louie
☐ Take Buster for a walk
☐ Clean room
☐ Do homework

To Do

Buy surprise-party invitations

. . . or like this.

☐ _____
☐ _____
☐ _____

Buy surprise party invitations

To Do

☐ Do homework
☐ Clean room

When it's unfolded, only you will know the special meaning in the markings.

Buy surprise party invitations

To Do

☐ Do homework
☐ Clean room
☐ Take Buster for a walk
☐ Call Grandpa Louie
☐

Fan mail is fun mail!

Here's a "cool" way to write on the edge.

These dots become a message when the fan is closed.

You will need:
- one sheet of unlined paper
- a marker
- a stapler

Step 1 Fold the paper back and forth to pleat it accordion-style.

Step 2 Pinch the pleats together to create an edge to write on. Then write your message in marker.

U R NiCE!

Step 3 Staple the fan near the bottom and open out the folds. Give the fan to a friend who's really "hot." Tell her to close it to see what she's got!

Pass it on.

Notes are easy to pass when they're folded into footballs.

Step 1 Write your note on a sheet of paper. Then fold the paper in half lengthwise . . .

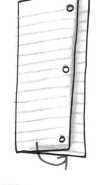

. . . and then again.

Step 2 Fold the top left corner down to the opposite edge.

54

Step 3 Fold that triangle down, lining up the right edges.

Step 4 Fold the top right corner down to the opposite edge.

Step 5 Fold this triangle down, lining up the left edges.

Step 6 Keep folding in this way until you can't complete another whole triangle.

Step 7 Fold a corner of the remaining paper up to the base of the triangle.

Step 8 Tuck this flap up into the open end of the triangle.

Pass your paper football to your "receiver," or send it through the goal for extra points.

55

For a **SPECIAL DELIVERY**, turn your note into its own envelope and drop it off yourself.

Step 1 Write your note on one side of a sheet of paper. Then turn the paper sideways, with the side you've written on facing up.

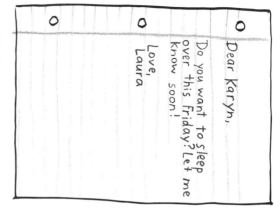

Step 2 Fold both top corners down so that they meet in the middle.

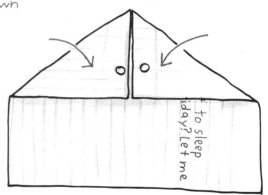

TIP: Run your thumbnail along the creases as you fold. This will keep your paper folded and give you a crisp-looking envelope.

more

Step 3 Fold the bottom edge up so that it meets the bottom edge of the triangle.

Step 4 Then fold the bottom up again at the base of the triangle.

Step 5 Fold in the sides so they overlap and so the edges are both the same distance from the top of the triangle.

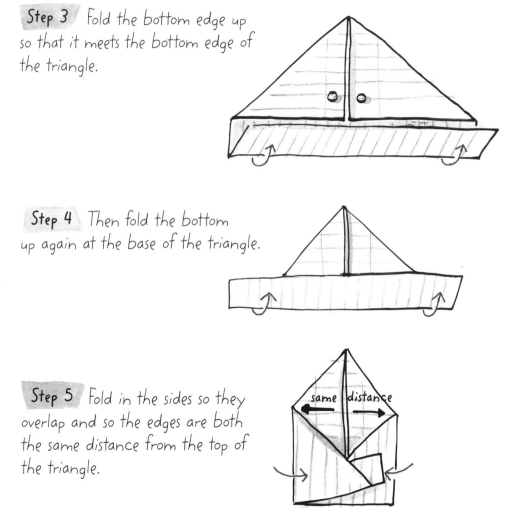

same distance

Step 6 Tuck one flap into the other.

Step 7 Fold the top point down and seal it with a sticker or a small piece of tape.

Before you hand-deliver your letter, have some fun making it look like real mail.

From: Laura Allen
Locker 292

WILMETTE, IL
PM
21 JAN
1997

To: Karyn Bertschi
Locker 238

HANDLE WITH CARE

FIRST CLASS MAIL

Girltown, USA
59

Make your next postcard a smooshing success!

Smoosh, smudge, smear, dab, or drip a few colorful souvenirs of special moments from your trip. Then tell the story behind each stain. Lots of things will leave a mark. See?

grass

mustard

cherry popsicle

blueberry pie

raspberry tea

dirt

toothpaste

sunblock

dandelion

deep dish pizza

TIP: You can even send something invisible, as long as it has a strong scent. Just tell your reader to "scratch 'n' sniff."

WARNING: Avoid getting stuck with a sticky postcard. Don't dab on things that won't dry!

Hi from camp Bugaboo. Had the best birthday ever!

← Smooshed petal from the crown of wildflowers my bunkmates gave me.

Mud from the lake where we went waterskiing! →

We ate chocolate cake around the campfire. I saved you some frosting. ←

Wax from the b-day candles (made for me in arts and crafts)! ←

Love and smooshes,
Jackie →

ps. Can you smell what this is?

It's bug spray!

To:
Laura Allen
245 Sunnyside Drive
Wilmette, IL 60091

Leave a paper trail.

Every day, on a separate paper strip, write a little bit about what happened on your trip . . .

. . . or, if you'd prefer, "picture" what you want to say. Then tape the strip on at the end of the day.

March 24
Dear Chloe,
We're finally on our way! I just wish we didn't have to drive for two days. (You-know-who is really bugging me.)

March 25
Today it was warm enough to eat lunch outside! Other than that, the trip is still boring.

March 26
It's hot here and there's a huge pool! I practiced my dives all day, even though you-know-who started calling me "the frog." He's the toad, if you ask me.

March 27
Me feeding dolphin →

freckles from sun

Wow!

Toad-boy was so impressed that he even stopped teasing me!

March 28 ～ Mom says that I should mail this letter today if I want it to reach you before I get home. I'll tell you about the rest of our trip in person. Love,
Zoe

Use accordion-style pleats when it comes time to fold it.
Then place it in an envelope that's large enough to hold it.

March 24
Dear Chloe,
We're finally on our way! I just wish
we didn't have to drive for two days.
(You-know-who is really bugging me.)

though you-know-who started calling
me "the frog." He's the toad, if you ask me.

IMPORTANT: If your letter is really thick and bulky, it may need more than one stamp. Take your letter to a post office or a hotel desk clerk to find out how much postage you need.

Sentence Scenery

These are the edges of the big, dark thunder-

Rain, rain, rain, rain! It's been raining almost nonstop here. Since it's the slanty kind, you can't even keep dry with

The waves are really high, to sleep with them crashing they look. But Steve says At least the fish like the weather. I suppose that's because they're all wet anyway. which is all night. I they look that way

A picture may paint a thousand words,
but words can also paint a picture.

clouds that have been hanging over us for days.

an umbrella.

Yesterday, we

thought that it

had finally

stopped.

So we went

out for a walk.

Big mistake!

exciting

even

So here I am, staring out the window, wondering if I'll ever get to go sailing. At least I'm winning at cards, building lots of fires, and reading a really great mystery. Even though it's kinda cozy here, I still can't wait for the rain to stop so we can set sail.

though it's hard

was surprised

'cuz they're

Love

at how brown

churning up sand.

Laura

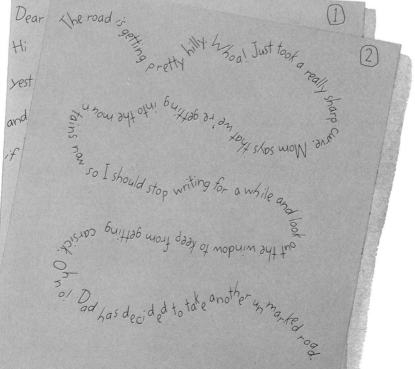

Lookout Point 1 mi.

Take your reader along for the ride. . .

Run your words up and down hills. Twist them around hair-pin turns.

Jostle the letters to show bumps in the road.

Dear
Hi
yest
and
if

①
②

The road is getting pretty hilly. Whoa! Just took a really sharp curve. Mom says that we're getting into the mountains now so I should stop writing for a while and look out the window to keep from getting carsick. Oh no! Dad has decided to take another unmarked road.

68

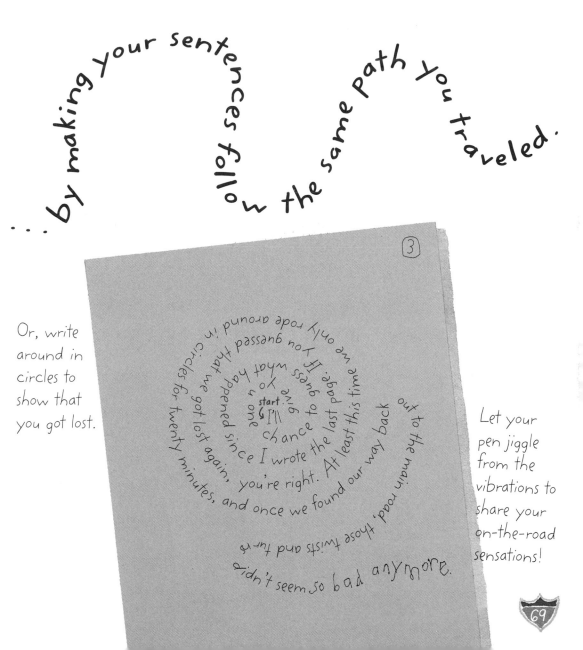

...by making your sentences follow the same path you traveled.

③

Or, write around in circles to show that you got lost.

I'll give you one chance to guess what happened since I wrote the last page. If you guessed that we got lost again, you're right. At least this time we only rode around in circles for twenty minutes, and once we found our way back out to the main road, those twists and turns didn't seem so bad anymore.

Let your pen jiggle from the vibrations to share your on-the-road sensations!

Create a clever communication
by recycling the papers
from your vacation.

Recycle
menus, place mats,
shopping bags,
road and trail maps,
pamphlets, brochures,
programs, wrapping
paper, etc.

The back of a paper
place mat is perfect
for a letter.

Dear Grace,
This very place mat sat underneath the
biggest meal I think I've ever eaten. But after our
hike today, I needed it! They call this place "The
Big House," but we all ate so much that now
we're calling it "The Pig House." I laughed so
hard making oinking noises in the car that

My Bananza Burger
was messy but delicious!

70

Use pictures from brochures you would have thrown away to show your friends where you went each day.

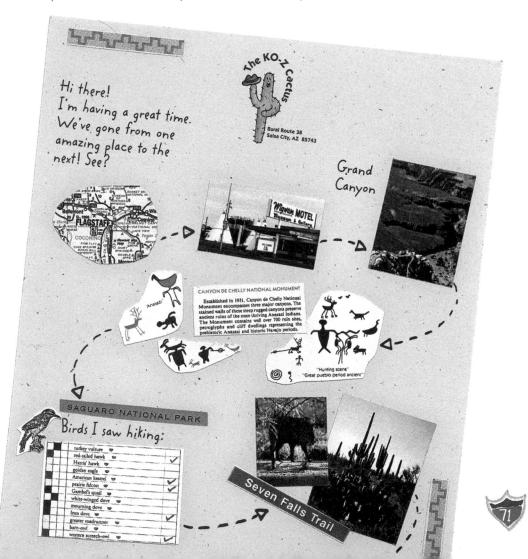

The KO-Z Cactus

Rural Route 38
Salsa City, AZ 85743

Hi there!
I'm having a great time.
We've gone from one amazing place to the next! See?

FLAGSTAFF
COCONINO

Wigwam MOTEL
Museum & Gallery

Grand Canyon

CANYON DE CHELLY NATIONAL MONUMENT

Established in 1931, Canyon de Chelly National Monument encompasses three major canyons. The stained walls of these steep rugged canyons preserve ancient ruins of the once thriving Anasazi Indians. The Monument contains well over 700 ruin sites, petroglyphs and cliff dwellings representing the prehistoric Anasazi and historic Navajo periods.

'Anasazi'

"Hunting scene"
"Great pueblo period ancient"

SAGUARO NATIONAL PARK

Birds I saw hiking:

turkey vulture		
red-tailed hawk		✓
Harris' hawk		
golden eagle		
American kestrel		✓
prairie falcon		
Gambel's quail		
white-winged dove		
mourning dove		
Inca dove		✓
greater roadrunner		
barn-owl		
western screech-owl		✓

Seven Falls Trail

Turn a map you no longer need into an envelope that's fun to read.

Stacey Rosen
2, rue de la Plume
Paris 75004
FRANCE

PAR AVION

This is French for "airmail."

You will need:

- an unused envelope
- an old road map or trail map
- a pencil
- scissors
- glue
- a white mailing label

Step 1 Gently peel apart the glued flaps of the unused envelope and unfold it.

Step 2 Lay the unfolded envelope facedown on the road map and trace around it. Then cut the envelope shape out of the map.

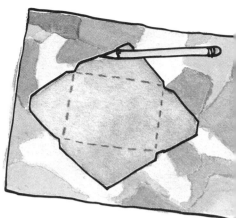

Step 3 Fold and glue this cutout shape in all the same places the original envelope was folded and glued.

Fold in the sides first.

Dab a little glue along the bottom edges.

Then fold the bottom up.

Step 4 Put your letter inside and glue the top flap down. Stick the mailing label on the front. Write your friend's address on the label, then add a stamp and send the letter on its way.

Bon voyage!

US Mail

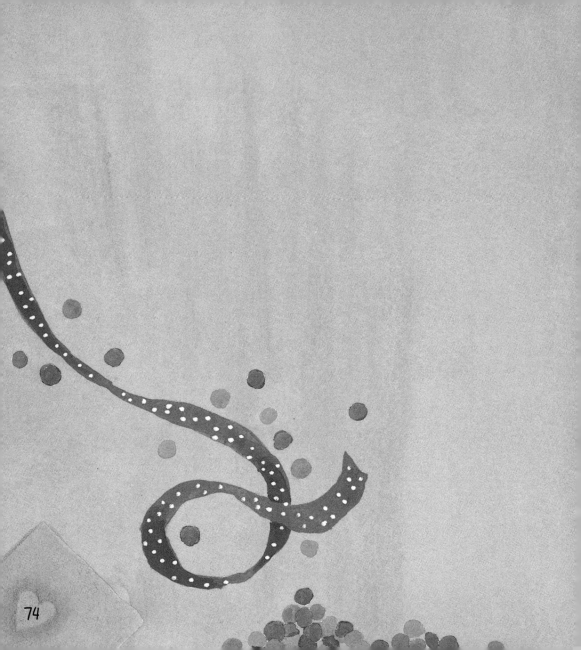

Spatter on spots
to make speckled stationery.

Dip an old toothbrush into some watered-down ink or paint. Then spatter the paint onto a piece of paper by flicking the bristles with your thumb or fingers.

WARNING: The paint will fly farther than you think. Spread lots of newspaper around and, if possible, do this outside or in a large, dry sink.

Dip and dab
for a look that's never drab.

Step 1 Dip a ball of crinkled-up plastic wrap into a small amount of light-colored ink or paint.

Step 2 Blot the ball on scrap paper until it stops leaving glops.

Step 3 Dab repeatedly on the sheet of paper you want to decorate. Keep dipping and dabbing until the page is lightly covered.

Try using several different colors, including metallic paints.

Cut a zigzag edge with pinking shears.

Dark colors are harder to write on. You'll probably need to use a black marker.

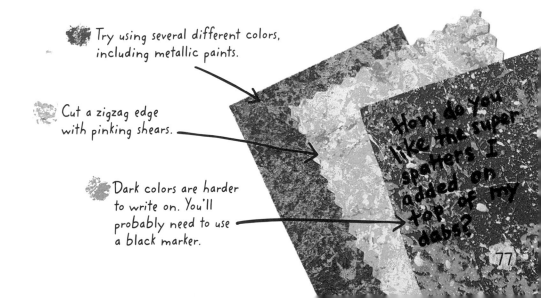

How do you like the super spatters I added on top of my dabs?

77

Glue on sections of rickrack, then decorate them with colored pencils to make roosters.

Carve footprints out of potatoes, then stamp your feet around!

Dress up your edges...

then punch holes and weave ribbon through it. Tie the ends in a bow.

Even grocery bag paper can look fancy. Cut it out with pinking shears,

Use scraps of gift wrap to piece together a patterned frame.

Color in a row of your favorite rubber stamp prints.

...with unbeatable borders.

Turn a line of loops into silly, swirly girls!

Leave a trace of LACE.

Step 1 Place the doily on the paper where you want the design to appear.

Step 2 Dip your brush in the paint and dab off any extra on the scrap paper so that the bristles are just lightly coated.

Step 3 Hold the doily in place with one hand. With the other, dab the paint into the holes, using short, quick strokes. Peel off the doily.

Grace your space with *artsy* add-ons.

Cut a small shape out of paper. Color it heavily with pencil—especially near the edges. Place it on your stationery. Then use your finger to smudge the pencil over the edges onto the paper around it.

Look what an ink pad, markers, and one thumb or finger can do!

Write back soon!

Use pointed scissors to cut shutters into your paper. Tape a photo or drawing behind the window, then color around it.

Personalize your pages.

Use a computer to create your own professional-looking letterhead.

Most businesses have stationery called letterhead printed with their name, address, and other information. Experiment with type styles, borders, and spacing to create your own letterhead. My friend Millie designed these.

She uses this when she wants to be businesslike.

She uses this when she writes to her grandma.

She lets the real Millie come out when she writes to me.

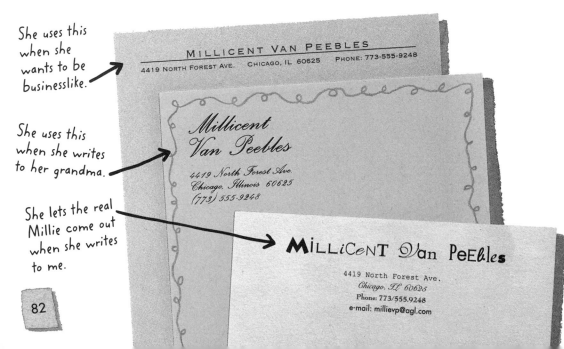

MILLICENT VAN PEEBLES
4419 NORTH FOREST AVE.   CHICAGO, IL 60625   PHONE: 773-555-9248

Millicent
Van Peebles
4419 North Forest Ave.
Chicago, Illinois 60625
(773) 555-9248

MiLLiCeNT Van PeEbles
4419 North Forest Ave.
Chicago, IL 60625
Phone: 773/555.9248
e-mail: millievp@agl.com

Make your mark with a monogram.

Put your middle initial at the end and your last initial in the middle, bigger than the others. If you have two parts to your last name, put both letters in the middle.

(for Laura Denise Allen)

(for Millicent Anne Van Peebles)

You can also make a metallic monogram to stick on your stationery. You'll need a gold foil seal, available at most office supply stores.

Step 1 Before you remove the backing, use pencil to write your monogram in outline letters on the front. Press hard.

Step 2 Turn the seal over and rub your pencil lightly over the backing to reveal the outlines of the letters. Fill them in, pressing very hard. This works best if you do it on a pile of paper.

Step 3 Turn the seal over to see if the letters are raised enough. If not, fill them in some more.

Do drop in!

Stuff your letter with leaves, petals, or other tiny tokens of friendship.

A penny for your thoughts?

A dime for your dreams?

giggle gum

Flavored with excite-mint!

Send a stick of gum with a handmade wrapper to let your friend know you're stuck on her.

84

It's just as fun to find a
fortune in an envelope as it
is to pull it from a cookie!

EXPECT THE UNEXPECTED TODAY.

Unused stamps can
be a colorful surprise—
and they may just hurry
your friend's replies.

85

Put your letter in a pretty petal envelope.

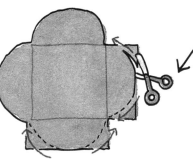

You will need:

- an 8" x 8" piece of colored paper
- a ruler
- a pencil
- scissors
- a sticker

Step 1 On the piece of colored paper, draw 4 lines, each 2 inches in from the edge, as shown.

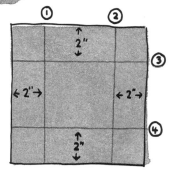

Step 2 Cut off each corner to leave 4 flaps.

Step 3 Round off each flap into a semicircle.

The best way to do this is to start from the outside and cut in toward the corners.

Step 4 Place your folded letter in the center. Starting with flap 1, fold each flap into the middle. Tuck the left edge of flap 4 underneath the top edge of flap 1.

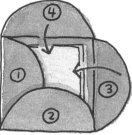 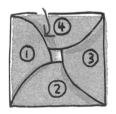

Step 5 Seal the envelope with a sticker. Then address it on the other side.

Send a special note in a Refined Lined Envelope

You will need:

- 2 unused envelopes the same size
- scissors
- a pencil
- gift wrap
- glue

Step 1 Gently peel apart the glued flaps of both envelopes to unfold them completely.

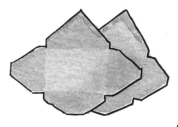

Step 2 On JUST ONE ENVELOPE, carefully cut off the left, right, and bottom flaps. Then cut off the strip you would normally lick.

Step 3 Lay the remaining piece on the gift wrap and trace around it.

88

Step 4 Cut out the traced shape and glue it onto the UNCUT envelope as shown.

Step 5 Refold and glue the envelope just as it was.

Fold in the sides first.

Dab a little glue along the bottom edges.

Then fold the bottom up.

Ta dah!

Now your envelope has inner beauty!

89

affectionately yours, bye for now, fondly, from, keep in touch,

wishing you were here, with love, write back soon, your friend...

until next time, very truly yours, waiting to hear from you,

with Style

looking forward to hearing from you, lots of love, love and kisses, missing you,

regards, see ya, sincerely, so long, thanks, thinking of you.

91

Creative Closings

People use these shortcuts to sign off on-line, but you can use them anywhere, anytime.

B4N (bye for now)

BBL (be back later)

CU (see you)

CUL8R (see you later)

TLK2UL8R or TTYL (talk to you later)

TAFN (that's all for now)

TTFN (ta-ta for now)

Any one of these closings is a great way to say "Friends 4-Ever" in a lighthearted way.

In a while, crocodile!

Yours till

. . . the ice screams

. . . the fire escapes

. . . Niagara Falls

. . . the fish bowls

. . . the tree barks

. . . the board walks

. . . the pencil points

. . . the bed spreads

. . . the autumn leaves

. . . the ocean waves

. . . the mouth of the Mississippi wears lipstick

. . . the refrigerator sees the salad dressing

Play name games.

See how many different ways you can write your signature.
Here are a few ideas to get you started.

This one "illustrates" (get it?) one of my favorite hobbies.

Leave a friend smiling by signing a fake name that sounds like something else when you say it out loud. You can use one of these names or make up your own.

Ann Chovey	Minnie Van Ryder	Anita Bath
Hazel Nutt	Patty O'Furniture	Harriet Upp
Chris P. Bacon	Lynn O'Leeum	I. M. Tired
Marsha Mellow	P. Anne O'Recital	I. Missy Ewe
Olive Yew	Ray O'Sun	Ivana B. Withew
Barb Akew	Isabelle Ringing	Anita Letterback
Aida Bugg	Eileen Sideways	Hope Furaletter
Maureen Biologist	Rita Book	I. Emma Dunn
Teri Dactyl	Paige Turner	B. Homesoon
Allie Gater	Rhoda Report	Bea Mine
Liz Erd	Augusta Wind	Bess Twishes
A. Mused	Chris Anthemum	C. Yasoon
Constance Noring	Anne Teak	Audie Yose
Lois Di Nominator	U. R. Nice	Dee End

You might use this one when you're writing from the road.

95

When all is said and done,
There's one more chance for fun.
Let your envelope have its say,
Then send it on its merry way.

Please handle me gently—
I'm really stuffed.

I'm bursting to tell you
what this letter says,
but my lips are sealed.

Bananas are yellow,
Chocolate is brown,
I sealed this envelope
Upside down!

I've been dropped, stamped, sorted,
and squooshed. I'm glad I'm here
'cuz boy I'm bushed.

Clever Letters

Fun ways to "wiggle" your words

By Laura Allen

Illustrated by Valerie Coursen

PLEASANT COMPANY PUBLICATIONS

Published by Pleasant Company Publications
© 1997 by Pleasant Company

Printed in the United States of America.
98 99 00 01 02 KRH 10 9 8 7 6 5 4 3

Editorial Development: Andrea Weiss
Art Direction and Design: Stacey Caplan
Photography: Jamie Young

Page 71: Flagstaff map, Rand McNally; Tucson Mountains Trail Map bird-watching checklist, Arizona Sonora Desert Museum; bird illustration, Ormsby and Thickstun Design; Canyon de Chelly National Monument description and pictures, North Star Mapping.
Page 72: United States map, the American Map Corporation, NY; Navajo and Hopi map, North Star Mapping.
Page 79: Vegetable stamps, ©Rubber Stampede Petite Stamp Set 740.04.

Library of Congress Cataloging-in-Publication Data
Allen, Laura. Clever letters : fun ways to wiggle your words / by Laura Allen ; illustrated by Valerie Coursen. — 1st ed.
p.   cm. "American girl library."
Summary: Introduces several lettering styles and secret message writing systems, and provides instructions for making decorative stationery and other paper crafts.
ISBN 1-56247-528-2
1. Paper work—Juvenile literature.   2. Lettering—Juvenile literature.   3. Stationery—Juvenile literature. [1. Paper work. 2. Lettering. 3. Handicraft.]   I. Coursen, Valerie, ill.
II. American girl (Middleton, Wis.)   III. Title.
TT870.A42 1997 745.6—dc21 97-12893   CIP AC